RAND

An Economic Framework for Evaluating Military Aircraft Replacement

Victoria A. Greenfield, David M. Persselin

Prepared for the United States Air Force

Project AIR FORCE

The research reported here was sponsored by the United States Air Force under Contract F49642-01-C-0003. Further information may be obtained from the Strategic Planning Division, Directorate of Plans, Hq USAF.

ISBN: 0-8330-3122-8

Published 2002 by RAND
1700 Main Street, P.O. Box 2138, Santa Monica, CA 90407-2138
1200 South Hayes Street, Arlington, VA 22202-5050
201 North Craig Street, Suite 102, Pittsburgh, PA 15213-1516
RAND URL: http://www.rand.org/
To order RAND documents or to obtain additional information, contact Distribution Services: Telephone: (310) 451-7002; Fax: (310) 451-6915; Email: order@rand.org

Preface

Aging aircraft, burdensome operating and support costs, and maintenance uncertainties have led the United States Air Force to ask when and how to replace its fleets. The Common Replacement Asset project within Project AIR FORCE's Aerospace Force Development program is assessing replacement policies for tanker and intelligence, surveillance, and reconnaissance (ISR) aircraft. This report describes some of the analysis done for this project. It presents an economic framework for identifying cost-effective aircraft replacement strategies. The framework recognizes tradeoffs among costs and explicitly incorporates the effects of age and uncertainty. It should be of interest to procurement analysts and policymakers.

This project was requested by General Michael Ryan, AF/CC, now retired. The primary Air Staff point of contact was Mr. Harry Disbrow, deputy AF/XOR.

This research was completed in July 2001.

Project AIR FORCE

Project AIR FORCE, a division of RAND, is the Air Force federally funded research and development center (FFRDC) for studies and analyses. It provides the Air Force with independent analyses of policy alternatives affecting the development, employment, combat readiness, and support of current and future aerospace forces. Research is performed in four programs: Aerospace Force Development; Manpower, Personnel, and Training; Resource Management; and Strategy and Doctrine.

Contents

Figures

Tables

Summary

Faced with concerns about aging aircraft, burdensome operation and support (O&S) costs, and maintenance uncertainties, the U.S. Air Force (USAF) is asking when and how to replace its fleets. Ultimately, the USAF must confront a broad range of economic and noneconomic considerations, including changes in technology and requirements. We focus primarily on economic considerations. Specifically, we develop an economic framework or model for identifying least-cost aircraft replacement strategies that recognizes tradeoffs among different kinds of costs and explicitly incorporates the effects of age and uncertainty. Our approach draws from studies of renewable resources, equipment replacement, industrial capacity expansion, and financial markets. For generality, we use the framework to conduct a parametric analysis.

We begin by developing a simple deterministic model that minimizes the life-cycle costs—acquisition and O&S—of an infinite series of replacements for a generic fleet of aircraft. In the deterministic model, O&S costs rise systematically with aircraft age. (Age is defined broadly to include other related factors, such as flying hours, sorties, and engine cycles.) The USAF repeats the replacement decision over and over again; each generation of the fleet becomes costlier to maintain as it ages, so that eventually it is retired and replaced. Holding technology, requirements, and other environmental factors constant, we can say that the replacement age or interval that is optimal for the first generation is optimal for all future generations. For illustrative purposes, we adopt a specific functional form—an exponential O&S cost growth process—and solve over a wide range of parameter values for the cost-minimizing replacement age. As the growth rate of O&S costs decreases, the optimal replacement interval lengthens, and the range of replacement intervals that provide close-to-optimal outcomes widens.

Next we add stochastic terms to the deterministic exponential growth process to incorporate two forms of uncertainty—one is continuous and the other is discrete. Of the many possible relationships between age and uncertainty, we focus on random events that are unrelated to age but affect the fleet differently as it ages. For example, an older fleet may be more susceptible to damage from an unanticipated increase in operational tempo than a newer fleet. We add a diffusion process to account for the possibility of continuous fluctuations in O&S costs and a jump process to account for permanent upward shifts in a generation's O&S cost function. The key uncertainty parameter in the diffusion process is the variance; for the jump process, the probability and magnitude of the shift characterize the uncertainty.

We find that the two stochastic processes have opposing and potentially offsetting effects on the optimal replacement strategy. By introducing the possibility of "good" and "bad" cost path realizations, the diffusion process serves to lengthen the optimal replacement interval and reduce life-cycle costs, but only slightly if the variance of the process is low relative to the expected growth rate. However, as the variance increases, all else constant, the effects of the diffusion process become more pronounced and the cost associated with setting policy according to a simple deterministic model becomes greater. This result suggests that the potential costs from failing to account for uncertainty will be greater in a high-variance system. In contrast, the jump process only serves to increase the effective rate of O&S cost growth. However, different combinations of jump probabilities and magnitudes can yield the same overall expected growth rate of O&S costs, but lead to somewhat different optimal strategies. In the combined jump-diffusion model, the net effect of the two processes depends on their relative strength, measured in terms of the underlying values of the uncertainty parameters.

When and how should the USAF replace its fleets of aircraft? Although a parametric analysis cannot provide a definitive answer, our results suggest that policymakers may have some leeway in choosing a replacement age. For low O&S cost growth rates, the USAF's total ownership costs stay within a narrow range of the minimum over extended periods. This leeway may be especially important if procurement budgets are constrained and may help free up funds for other acquisitions. However, as the growth rate in O&S costs rises, or the effects of jumps become larger, this kind of financing becomes more costly, measured by the deviation from the least-cost solution. Finally, the stochastic results suggest that the form of uncertainty matters. Observing the tension between the diffusion and jump processes, we find it especially important to be able to characterize the nature of the uncertainty—both qualitatively and quantitatively.

Acknowledgments

We are especially indebted to Michael Kennedy, the associate director of PAF's Aerospace Force Development program and the leader of the Common Replacement Asset project within that program. He played a key role in the development of the economic framework for evaluating military aircraft replacement, helping us to maintain a clear focus on the question at hand while contributing valuable insight to the larger set of policy issues. Michael Miller, who reviewed an early draft, provided technical and presentational suggestions that were essential in improving the final product. We also wish to thank our RAND and non-RAND colleagues—Thomas Hamilton, Gregory Hildebrandt, Ronald Lile, Lane Pierrot, and Raymond Pyles—for their always helpful and thought-provoking comments. Gregory Hildebrandt and Raymond Pyles also provided us with data that better informed our approach. We also thank our Air Staff action officer, Major Rob Faulk of AF/XORI, for his support. Ultimately, however, we take full responsibility for any errors or omissions.

1. Introduction

> We have to figure out when it stops making sense to fix some of these old airplanes and it would just be cheaper to buy a new one.
>
> General Michael Ryan, then U.S. Air Force Chief of Staff (2000)

> DoD [Department of Defense] may be able to allow some weapons to age indefinitely, although it may need to spend more on modifications or overhauls to do so. In many cases, modifying systems is cheaper than buying new ones, and in some cases it is much cheaper. And overhauls—which simply replace worn-out parts—are likely to be even less expensive than modifications.
>
> Lane Pierrot, Senior Analyst, Congressional Budget Office (1999)

> Most important, many of the problems associated with aging material have emerged with little or no warning. This raises the concern that an unexpected phenomenon may suddenly jeopardize an entire fleet's flight safety, mission readiness, or support costs. . . .
>
> Raymond Pyles, Senior Information System Scientist, RAND (1999)

Faced with concerns about aging aircraft, burdensome operating and support (O&S) costs,[1] and maintenance uncertainties, the U.S. Air Force (USAF) is asking when and how to replace its fleets.[2] Ultimately, it must confront a broad range of economic and noneconomic considerations, including changes in technology and requirements. We focus primarily on economic considerations, including tradeoffs among costs and the potential effects of uncertainty.

We begin by asking two questions. First, on the presumed relationship between age and costs, does aircraft aging contribute to higher and less-predictable O&S costs? Second, if so, can we model the essential features of that relationship to help the USAF identify an economically optimal replacement strategy?

Regarding the first question, we offer a cautious "yes." The weight of the evidence, discussed below, suggests that age contributes to higher O&S costs and, through a variety of direct and indirect channels, uncertainty. (Here, we

---

[1]Throughout this report, we are concerned with *aircraft* O&S costs; others sometimes refer to equipment or military O&S costs more generally.

[2]In 1998, then Under Secretary of Defense for Acquisition, Technology, and Logistics Jacques Gansler coined the phrase "death spiral," referring to his concerns that rising maintenance costs would crowd out modernization. His comments are reprinted in U.S. General Accounting Office (2000b), p. 6. See also then Secretary of the Air Force, F. Whitten Peters (2000).

define age broadly to include other related factors, such as flying hours, sorties, and engine cycles.) As aircraft mature beyond their planned service lives, their maintenance needs may become less predictable. Corrosion, for example, may require additional inspections and repairs.[3] Aircraft may also become less resilient with age, so that random events pose increasingly serious maintenance challenges.

Age—even broadly defined—is not the only relevant cost factor. Other factors, such as workforce reductions, depot closures, and spare parts shortages, may account for higher O&S costs. These kinds of structural, institutional, and systemic changes can push costs upward, sometimes unexpectedly.

Regarding the second question, we assert that an economic framework can help the USAF develop a more systematic approach to decisionmaking.[4] Cost tradeoffs and uncertainty suggest that the replacement problem lends itself naturally to economic modeling. In this report, we develop an economic framework for identifying optimal replacement strategies that recognizes tradeoffs among costs and explicitly incorporates uncertainty. For generality, we use the framework to conduct a parametric analysis. Were we modeling a particular aircraft type, we would use platform-specific parameter values.

In Section 2, the literature review, we observe that aircraft replacement is a recurring investment decision and focus on asset replacement models and stochastic extensions. In Section 3, we develop a simple deterministic model, adopting a "Faustmann-like" framework to minimize the life-cycle costs—acquisition and O&S—of an infinite series of aircraft replacements. In Section 4, we introduce and develop a jump-diffusion process to account for continuous and discrete forms of uncertainty. Throughout Sections 3 and 4, we present quantitative illustrations. In each section, we identify an optimal replacement strategy for a generic fleet, ultimately comparing the least-cost solutions with and without uncertainty and testing the sensitivity of the results to key parametric assumptions. Finally, in Section 5, we evaluate policy implications and suggest opportunities for future research.

---

[3]See the National Research Council (1997) report on aging USAF aircraft.

[4]National Research Council (1997) cites the need for a comprehensive and credible methodology to account for the potential effects of corrosion, fatigue, and other cost factors in determining the economic service life of USAF aircraft.

2. Literature Review

Empirical evidence tends to suggest a positive relationship between aging and O&S costs for military aircraft. For example, RAND testimony, presented by Pyles (1999) before the U.S. Congress, shows heavy-maintenance workloads increasing with chronological age for the KC-135 tanker and several commercial aircraft, roughly on the order of five- to ninefold over a 40-year span, but it does not statistically isolate the effects of age (see Figure 1 for KC-135 data).[1] That same testimony also cites the results of previous RAND research on engine support costs, reporting annual age-driven growth rates of 4.5 to 5.3 percent for depot- and base-level engine repairs, respectively.

In an earlier RAND study, Hildebrandt and Sze (1990) estimate the effects of various explanatory factors on USAF aircraft O&S costs. They find that a one-

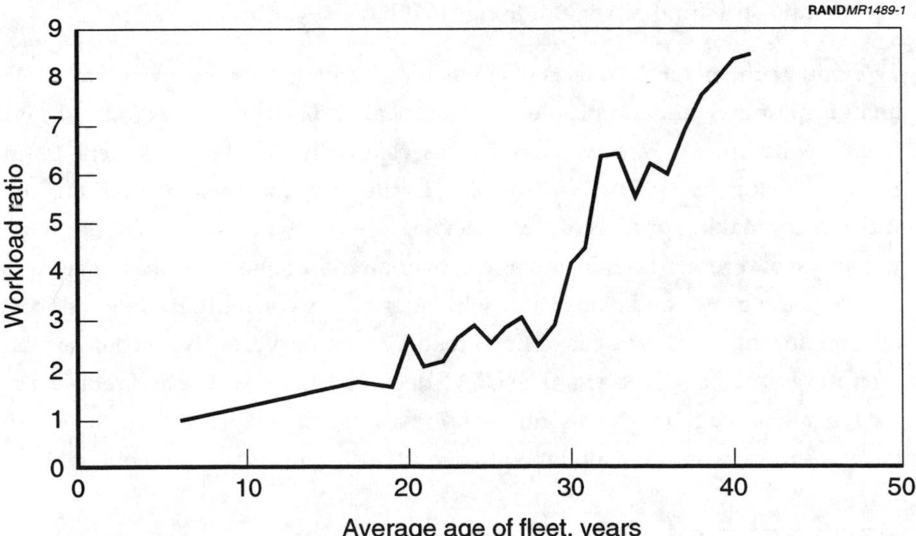

SOURCE: Data from Pyles (1999).

Figure 1—KC-135 Heavy-Maintenance Workload Ratio

[1]In an earlier analysis, Kenneth E. Marks and Ronald W. Hess (1981) find that costs tend to rise with age for some types of military aircraft. Mike Didonato and Greg Sweers (1997) provide more evidence on costs and aging for commercial aircraft.

year increase in the average age of a mission design series increases total O&S costs by about 1.7 percent. Of that figure, depot maintenance costs rose by about 2.6 percent, reflecting an increase in aircraft overhaul O&S costs of about 7.7 percent. Although generally supporting the later RAND testimony, these relations are estimated across all USAF aircraft types and would not be appropriately applied to a specific mission design.

U.S. General Accounting Office (GAO) and recent press reports also attribute higher costs to age, but do not provide statistical analyses.[2] A USAF-led KC-135 economic service life study is expected to provide additional data and references; it has not yet been publicly released.[3]

Regarding uncertainty, the RAND testimony cited above notes that "many of the problems associated with aging material have emerged with little or no warning," but quantitative evidence on costs is largely anecdotal. For example, a recent press report from Wolf (2001), "Air Force Estimates Need for $500M to Fix Unanticipated Equipment Problems," quotes then Air Force Vice Chief of Staff General John Handy: "things that are breaking on our weapons systems aren't the predictable parts that you have engineered predictions on. Now we are getting into structural repair and things that have never broken before."

To evaluate the potential effects of aging and uncertainty, we develop an analytical framework and proceed parametrically. The framework draws heavily from the literature on renewable resources, especially forest management, dating back to Faustmann (1849). Why forests? To illustrate the analogy, first consider the decisionmaking process of a commercial forester. The forester decides when to harvest and replant, again and again, over an infinite horizon. Each new timber stand grows and gains value with age; all else constant, the interval that is optimal for the first harvest is optimal for all future harvests. Now consider the aircraft replacement problem. The USAF decides when to retire and replace its fleet, again and again, over an infinite horizon.[4] Each new generation of aircraft becomes more costly to maintain with age; all else constant, the interval that is

[2]See U.S. General Accounting Office (1996) and various press reports, e.g., John A. Tirpak (2000).

[3]The research for our study was completed prior to the publication of U.S. Congressional Budget Office (2001), *The Effects of Aging on the Costs of Operating and Maintaining Military Equipment.* That report, which includes a review of several other previous empirical studies, estimates that spending on operating and maintenance (O&M) for aircraft increases by 1–3 percent for every additional year, after adjusting for inflation. Their estimate for aircraft O&M spending appears to be roughly in line with the empirical studies we cite; however, owing to methodological differences, these and other estimates may be difficult to compare directly.

[4]We assume that the USAF faces an infinite security requirement. Because aircraft are not infinitely lived, this, in turn, implies an infinite series of replacements. Another approach to solving this type of problem is to assume that there is one replacement and that it is infinitely long-lived. We later compare one-time replacement and repeated replacement optimality results.

optimal for the first replacement is optimal for all future replacements.[5] Both the forester and the USAF face a recurring investment decision.

Other researchers outside the resource community have either wittingly or unwittingly used this approach and we will discuss some of their modifications, extensions, and insights below.

The Underlying Methodology

Faustmann generally receives credit for describing the commercial forester's problem as a recurring investment decision. His formulation provides a basic insight: The present-value sum of net revenues received at each rotation over an infinite series of rotations can be concisely stated as a geometric series. Maximization of the geometrically stated present-value sum with respect to the length of the rotation interval yields an optimality condition known as the Faustmann equation. As economic theory predicts, the equation tells the forester to choose the rotation interval that balances the marginal cost and benefit of extending the interval, where the benefit derives not just from the harvest value of the current stand but from the harvest value of all future stands.

Apparently, Faustmann's insight was slow in filtering to the general economics and finance literature.[6] Nevertheless, a related, if sometimes independent, body of research emerged over the next several decades, beginning with one-time machinery replacement models, such as those produced by Taylor (1923) and Hotelling (1925). Preinreich (1940) later extends the Taylor and Hotelling formulations and develops a more Faustmann-like approach by using the geometric series to describe an infinite series of industrial equipment replacements.

Other researchers have applied these kinds of techniques to military equipment replacement. Alchian's (1952, 1958) replacement study for the USAF, which seeks to determine an equipment replacement policy that minimizes present-value cost over an infinite horizon, also employs the geometric series formulation.[7] He provides a numerical solution.[8] Hildebrandt (1980) extends

---

[5] Although we adopt an "all else constant" specification, this approach can be modified to accommodate differences between the current system and the follow-on systems.

[6] M. Gane comments on the "failure of communications" in his introduction to the first English language translation of Faustmann's paper. See M. Gane (1968).

[7] We note that other military researchers have performed cost-benefit analyses. Two examples are Boness and Schwartz' (1969) study of F-9J trainer aircraft replacement and Schwartz, Sheler, and Cooper's (1971) study of F-4A fighter aircraft replacement.

[8] Others, such as Bellman (1955) and Dreyfus (1960), use dynamic programming to numerically solve other related replacement problems.

Alchian's equipment replacement model by considering the cost of age-induced performance deterioration. Hildebrandt notes, however, that some types of military equipment may not experience performance deterioration "because of the required maintenance activities that keep the equipment at the original efficiency level." We adopt this constant performance perspective in our treatment of life-cycle costs.

Contributing to the empirical literature, Smith (1957) uses the geometric series replacement model and data on the trucking industry to estimate the profit-maximizing truck replacement age. He finds that profit is relatively insensitive to the replacement interval and notes that, as a consequence, delayed replacement can help fund the trucking fleet's expansion. In the aircraft context, Smith's finding suggests that the USAF might be able to delay aircraft replacement beyond the optimum at little additional cost to temporarily free-up funds for other acquisition purposes.

Adding Uncertainty to the Model

Beginning with Manne (1961), a series of industrial, resource, and other models elaborate on stochastic properties and provide insight on the potential effects of uncertainty on the optimal replacement interval.

Manne breaks new ground in a capacity expansion model by introducing a diffusion process into the geometric series—he treats stochastic demand as a simple Brownian motion. Manne recognizes and frames this problem as one of an "expected first passage time" to the next expansion, wherein demand rises to a threshold or trigger level, signaling that another expansion is optimal.[9] Manne uses mathematical techniques described in Feller (1957) to write a geometric series of costs in terms of both the mean and the variance of demand.

Meyer (1971) extends Manne's approach to equipment replacement using a simple Brownian motion to describe the cost savings achievable through replacement. Comparing his stochastic result with the result from a deterministic model, Meyer finds the expected cost savings from using a stochastic model are significant if the variance is high relative to the mean growth rate of cost savings. Returning to the forestry literature, Miller and Voltaire (1983) contribute a similar treatment of the forest rotation problem when tree value follows a simple Brownian motion.

---

[9]This is also known as the problem of the "gambler's ruin."

Of direct application to our research, Willassen (1998) updates Miller and Voltaire and derives optimality conditions for the cases of tree growth following simple and geometric Brownian motions. We extend Willassen to model aircraft replacement when O&S costs follow a geometric Brownian motion, but add random proportional jumps as described in Dixit and Pindyck (1994). Although Willassen's work on stochastic processes follows the general approach outlined in Oksendal (1998), our approach is closer to that discussed in Hertzler (1991) and well illustrated in Dixit and Pindyck. Specifically, we set up a recursive Bellman equation for the expected present-value life-cycle costs of a generation of aircraft, use Ito's lemma to expand it into a differential equation, and then solve the differential equation to obtain a closed-form expression. We discuss this solution methodology in Appendix A.

3. Deterministic Model

In this analysis, we identify the optimal, i.e., least-cost, replacement strategy for a fleet of aircraft, holding technology and requirements constant.[1]

The deterministic model incorporates three kinds of cost: acquisition p, operating and support m, and capital r. For simplicity, we assume that any extraordinary O&S costs that are incurred during an initial "shake-out" period are reflected in the fleet's acquisition cost; therefore, we specify m as a continuously increasing function of the fleet's age, so that $m = m(a)$.[2] Retirement and replacement occur simultaneously and payment is instantaneous.[3] Given p, $m(a)$, and r, the USAF seeks to replace each generation of aircraft so as to minimize total ownership costs over an infinite time horizon.[4] Accordingly, the USAF owns an infinitely long series of aircraft generations.

Consider the present-value life-cycle costs of the first generation of aircraft. At time zero the USAF purchases a new fleet. It then pays O&S costs until the generation is retired and replaced, at which time the cycle starts over. Let s be the age of the first generation when it is retired or scrapped and replaced.[5] We write the present-value life-cycle cost of this generation as

$$p + \int_0^s m(a)e^{-ra}da \tag{1}$$

The replacement process repeats itself ad infinitum. Because, in this model, the USAF faces the same life-cycle costs for each new generation of aircraft, the optimal replacement interval or age is the same for all generations. Indexing each replacement in the series by i, we can express the total cost of the infinite

---

[1]We do not address aircraft availability directly, but note that the evidence on trends in mission capable rates is somewhat murky. For examples of different perspectives on these rates, see the U.S. General Accounting Office (2000a) and F. Whitten Peters (2000).

[2]Chronological age a is a rough proxy for flying hours, sorties, and engine cycles. In a more elaborate model, we would model each of these factors separately.

[3]In reality, research and development (R&D) and other acquisition cost spreading occurs over time.

[4]For the purpose of this analysis, we define total ownership costs as the total present-value cost—acquisition and O&S—of owning all generations of a fleet. Since most of the total ownership costs accumulate during the first acquisition cycle in our model, there is little practical difference between finite- and infinite-horizon specifications. Note, however, that a finite-horizon specification would be more appropriate if the planning horizon were quite short or the growth rate of O&S costs quite high.

[5] The scrapping value in this model is zero, but a fixed scrapping value, either positive or negative, could be subtracted from the purchase price.

series of replacements as the discounted sum of each of the individual generation life-cycle costs:

$$c(s) = \sum_{i=0}^{\infty} (p + \int_0^s m(a)e^{-ra}da)e^{-rsi} \tag{2}$$

Recognizing that this type of infinite process is a geometric series, we can rewrite the USAF's total ownership cost, i.e., the total present-value cost of acquiring, operating, and supporting all generations of a fleet, as[6]

$$c(s) = \frac{p + \int_0^s m(a)e^{-ra}da}{1 - e^{-rs}} \tag{3}$$

From this total cost function we differentiate with respect to s, equate to zero, and thus derive the optimality condition:

$$m(s^*) = rp + r\frac{\int_0^{s^*} m(a)e^{-ra}da + pe^{-rs^*}}{1 - e^{-rs^*}} \tag{4}$$

where s^* is the optimal replacement interval. Simply put, the USAF should retire and replace the fleet when the marginal cost of further retention just equals the marginal benefit. Shown here on the right-hand side (RHS) of Eq. (4), the marginal benefit consists of the present-value saving, measured in terms of the cost of funds, from deferring the purchase of the next generation and all future generations of the fleet. For a one-time replacement, the second term on the RHS of Eq. (4) drops out, leaving $m(s^*) = rp$.

For illustrative purposes, we adopt a specific functional form for $m(a)$ and solve numerically. Let O&S costs evolve exponentially, so that $m(a) = be^{\alpha a}$, where b is the instantaneous O&S cost of a new aircraft generation, i.e., the initial cost at age $a = 0$, and α is the growth rate of O&S costs.[7]

For the exponential form, the total cost function and optimality condition are

$$c(s) = \frac{p + \dfrac{b(1 - e^{-(r-\alpha)s})}{r - \alpha}}{1 - e^{-rs}} \tag{5}$$

[6]A geometric series, $a + ab + ab^2 + \ldots$, converges if $|b| < 1$. When the series converges, the sum can be represented as $a/(1 - b)$. In our example, the present-value life-cycle cost equation takes the place of the constant a, and e^{-rs} takes the place of the constant b. Note that $|e^{-rs}| < 1$, so the geometric series of present-value life-cycle costs converges and can be written as in Eq. (3).

[7]Looking at the data in Figure 1, the exponential specification provides a reasonable fit. We are comparing the results of linear and concave functional forms in another study.

and

$$m(s^*) = be^{\alpha s^*} = rp + r\frac{\dfrac{b(1-e^{-(r-\alpha)s^*})}{r-\alpha} + pe^{-rs^*}}{1-e^{-rs^*}} \tag{6}$$

As above, the USAF would equate the marginal costs and benefits of delaying replacement or, equivalently, extending the interval. Although the model does not yield a closed-form solution, we can solve for s^* both graphically and numerically. Because Eq. (6) is linear in p and b, proportional changes in p and b will wash out. Thus, p/b provides a basis for quantitative analysis.

First, we obtain the solution graphically by plotting the total cost equation as a function of s. Figure 2 illustrates the procedure for $\alpha = 0.025$ and $\alpha = 0.05$. In both of these examples, $r = 0.03$, $p/b = 50$, and $b = 1$, a normalized index. We are using $r = 0.03$ to approximate the Office of Management and Budget (OMB) rate.[8] We test the sensitivity of the results to this assumption in Appendix B.

The range of strategies that provides close to optimal outcomes narrows as the growth rate of O&S costs increases. In Figure 2, replacement ages between 29

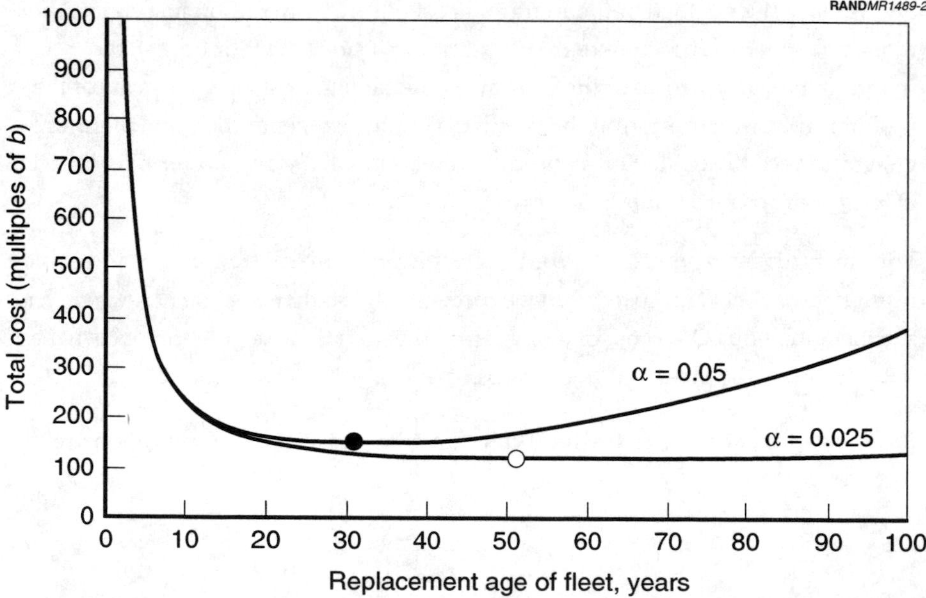

Figure 2—Graphical Solutions for the Deterministic Age-Based Model

[8]For purposes of cost-effectiveness analysis, OMB (2001) specifies 3.2 percent.

and 94, a range of 66 years after rounding, result in total costs that fall within 10 percent of the minimum when the growth rate, α, is 0.025. (This range is asymmetrically positioned around the cost-minimizing age, i.e., 52 years, suggesting that the USAF has somewhat more leeway in the out years of fleet management. That is, the consequences of replacing too late are less severe than replacing too soon.) By way of comparison, the range shrinks to 27 years when the growth rate increases to 0.05. Though not obvious in Figure 2, the majority of all costs accumulate during the first acquisition cycle, about 79 percent for α = 0.025 and 60 percent for α = 0.05.

Using a tool like *Mathematica*, we can also solve the model numerically.[9]

Table 1 provides intuitively appealing results. As the O&S growth rate increases, the optimal replacement interval decreases, and as the price-cost ratio increases, the optimal interval increases. See Appendix B for comparisons of the Table 1 results with results using lower and higher discount rates.

In the deterministic model, the exponential specification of O&S costs as a function of time ensures a one-to-one correspondence between age and O&S costs. Thus, we can define the replacement process in terms of either the age or level of O&S costs at which each generation is replaced. In the next section, which considers stochastically evolving costs, this one-to-one correspondence does not exist. At each age, the level of O&S costs is described by a distribution instead of a single value. For these cases, the defining point of a replacement process is the level of O&S costs at which a generation is replaced rather than the age at which it is replaced.

Table 1

Numerical Solutions for s^* in the Deterministic Age-Based Model

Growth	Ratio of Purchase Cost to Initial O&S Cost (p/b)					
Rate, α	5	10	25	50	75	100
0.010	33.07	47.39	76.12	107.92	131.20	149.85
0.025	18.72	25.77	38.66	51.66	60.68	67.72
0.033	15.93	21.71	32.06	42.26	49.23	54.63
0.050	12.22	16.40	23.64	30.54	35.16	38.69
0.075	9.50	12.58	17.77	22.57	25.73	28.12
0.100	7.93	10.41	14.50	18.23	20.65	22.47
0.150	6.14	7.95	10.87	13.47	15.14	16.39
0.200	5.10	6.55	8.85	10.86	12.14	13.10

[9]See Wolfram (2001).

We end this section with a brief presentation of the cost-based model to provide a foundation for the stochastic analysis. Recalling the form of Eqs. (5) and (6) above, we find the analogous total cost function and optimality condition to be[10]

$$c(x) = \frac{p + \dfrac{b\left[1 - \left(\dfrac{b}{x}\right)^{\frac{r}{\alpha}-1}\right]}{r-\alpha}}{1 - \left(\dfrac{b}{x}\right)^{\frac{r}{\alpha}}} \tag{7}$$

and

$$x^* = rp + r\frac{\dfrac{b\left[1 - \left(\dfrac{b}{x^*}\right)^{\frac{r}{\alpha}-1}\right]}{r-\alpha} + p\left(\dfrac{b}{x^*}\right)^{\frac{r}{\alpha}}}{1 - \left(\dfrac{b}{x^*}\right)^{\frac{r}{\alpha}}}. \tag{8}$$

As in the age-based formulation, Eq. (8) tells us that the USAF should equate the marginal costs and benefits of delaying replacement. Here too we can solve both graphically and numerically. Figure 3 illustrates the graphical approach for $p/b = 50$, $r = 0.03$, and $b = 1$, an index.

Table 2 presents illustrative numerical results.

We conclude with a simple crosswalk between the age-based and cost-based solutions. To make a direct comparison, we can find the age at which a cost-based policy indicates replacement by solving $x^{-1}(a)$.[11]

$$a(x) = \frac{1}{\alpha}\ln\left(\frac{x}{b}\right) \tag{9}$$

---

[10]Writing the total cost function in terms of a critical O&S cost level requires a somewhat different mathematical approach. To summarize, we derive and solve the differential equation for $M(x; b)$, where $M(x; b)$ represents the present-value O&S cost of a generation and $M(x; b)$ is read as "the value of the function M when m evolves from its current level b to the policy determined level x." Described in terms of the O&S cost integral, the upper bound can be reframed as $a(x)$ and integrated as $M(x; m) = \int m(a)e^{-ra}da$ from 0 to $a(x)$. To solve, we let x go to infinity and write the present value of life-cycle O&S costs as a recursive Bellman equation where $M(x; m) = mda + e^{-rda}[M(x; m) + dM(x; m)]$.

[11]We write the inverse function of $m(a)$, substituting the specific level of O&S costs at which replacement occurs, x, for the general level m. This gives the age that a fleet will have reached at the time when its O&S costs have risen from the initial level b to the replacement level x.

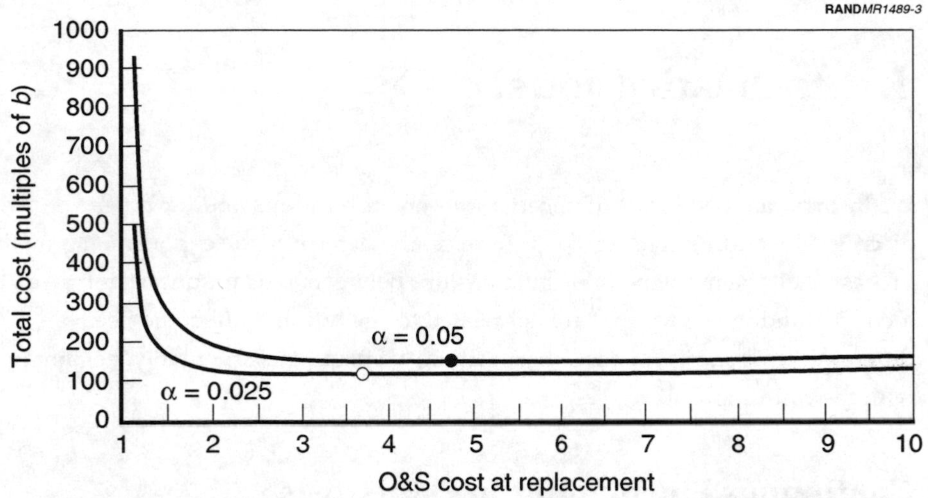

Figure 3—Graphical Solutions for the Deterministic Cost-Based Model

Table 2

Numerical Solutions for x^* in the Deterministic Cost-Based Model

Growth	Ratio of Purchase Cost to Initial O&S Cost (p/b)					
Rate, α	5	10	25	50	75	100
0.010	1.39	1.61	2.14	2.94	3.71	4.48
0.025	1.60	1.90	2.63	3.64	4.56	5.44
0.033	1.68	2.03	2.83	3.95	4.95	5.90
0.050	1.84	2.27	3.26	4.61	5.80	6.92
0.075	2.04	2.57	3.79	5.44	6.89	8.24
0.100	2.21	2.83	4.26	6.19	7.88	9.46
0.150	2.51	3.29	5.11	7.55	9.69	11.68
0.200	2.77	3.70	5.87	8.78	11.35	13.72

For $p/b = 50$ and $\alpha = 0.025$, Figure 3 and Table 2 indicate that x^*, the critical level of O&S costs, is about 3.64. Applying Eq. (9), the crosswalk suggests that s^* is about 51.7, as identified previously in Table 1.

Later, we will provide crosswalks for the stochastic model. However, absent a one-to-one correspondence between O&S costs and age, we will need to derive an expression for the expected age at which O&S costs reach x^*.

4. Stochastic Model

We incorporate two forms of uncertainty—one continuous and the other discrete—by adding two stochastic terms to the deterministic exponential growth process.[1] Of the many possible relationships between age and uncertainty, we focus on random events that are not related to age but that affect the fleet differently as it ages. For ease of exposition, we proceed sequentially, beginning with the continuous form.

Continuous Fluctuations in O&S Costs

We add a stochastic term to the exponential growth process to account for the possibility of continuous fluctuations in O&S costs. Such fluctuations may occur for any number of reasons having nothing to do with the age of the fleet, such as a change in operational tempo. We specify this form of uncertainty as a geometric Brownian motion—a type of diffusion process in which the instantaneous percentage changes in cost are distributed normally and the realized costs are distributed log-normally. Noting that $dm = \alpha m da$ is a restatement of the deterministic exponential growth process, we add $\sigma m dz$ to form the geometric Brownian motion:

$$dm = \alpha m da + \sigma m dz \tag{10}$$

In Eq. (10), α is the expected rate of change in O&S costs per unit age, dz is the increment of a Weiner process, and σ is the standard deviation of the change in costs per unit age.[2] (Note that O&S costs m cannot rebound from zero. Zero is an absorbing barrier. Alternatively, we could have specified a reflecting barrier at zero. However, sensitivity analysis for O&S cost growth rates ranging from 0.025 to 0.10 shows little difference in the result.) The random events in this model are not related to the age of the fleet, but their effects evolve proportionally with age. We can explain this process in terms of a fleet's

---

[1]The types of random events that we are considering as contributing to changes in O&S costs are related only to the current generation of the fleet, so that at replacement O&S costs return to the initial level. In effect, the O&S clock resets itself at each replacement. We do not address permanent changes in institutional features of the maintenance process that may persist across generations. These will be considered in another report.

[2]The expected value of a Weiner process is zero and the square of a Weiner increment is da.

resiliency—as a fleet ages, it becomes more susceptible to damage from random events. The purchase cost p, initial instantaneous O&S cost b, and government discount rate r are defined as previously.

To gain intuition, we have plotted in Figure 4 two realizations of O&S cost paths and compared them with the expected cost path. Note that the expected cost path, the smooth center curve, is the same as the deterministic exponential cost path described in the previous section. The cost path realizations were generated for $\sigma = 0.05$, $\alpha = 0.025$, and $b = 1$. These realizations are purely illustrative, demonstrating only two of the infinitely many possible paths that O&S costs could follow.

Recall that two factors influence the realized cost path in this model. The first factor is the fleet's age and the second is the series of random events. These events are weighted by σ, the standard deviation of O&S cost growth. Thus, as σ goes to zero, the influence of the events also goes to zero. If the predominant effect of the random events is to increase costs, the realized cost path will increase above the expected cost path as uncertainty increases. If the predominant effect is to decrease costs, the realized cost path will decrease below the expected cost path as uncertainty increases.

Although we expect to find 95 percent of all realizations of the cost path within the confidence interval shown in Figure 4, a cost path realization could remain

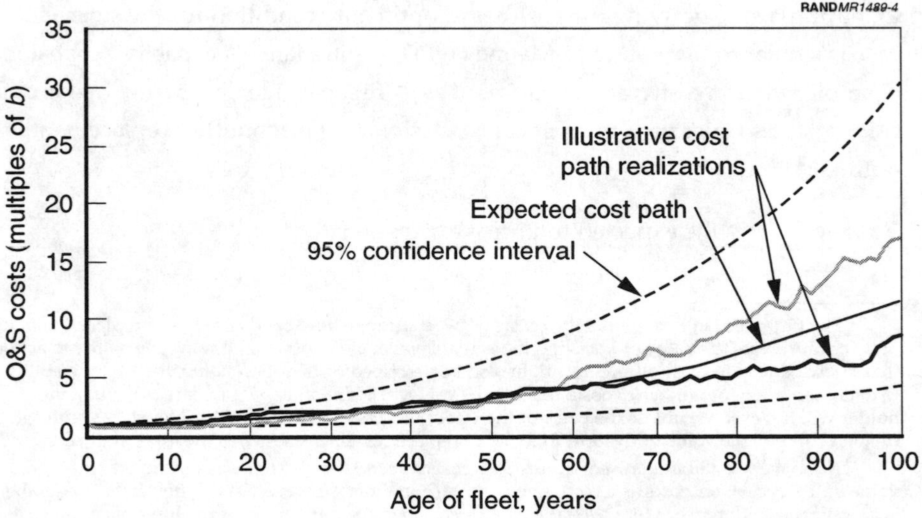

Figure 4—Two O&S Cost Path Realizations for the Diffusion Process

far from the expected path for a long time, or even forever. For this reason, it is important to recognize that the optimal replacement policy developed in what follows is optimal only in the sense that it minimizes the expectation of total cost. With hindsight, in light of the actual realized cost path, it may not have been the least-cost solution.

Life-Cycle Costs and Optimality Conditions

Recalling the optimality condition in Eq. (8), the USAF minimizes its total ownership costs by replacing each generation of the fleet when its marginal O&S costs first reach a critical level x^*. In the deterministic case, we can use age as a measure of the O&S cost level because age and O&S costs exhibit a one-to-one correspondence. As such, the age-based replacement policy is as effective at minimizing total ownership costs as the cost-based replacement policy.

In the stochastic case, there is no longer a one-to-one correspondence between age and O&S costs. Instead, at each age, the level of O&S costs is described by a probability distribution. Under an age-based replacement policy, the actual level of O&S costs at replacement could be above or below the critical level, thereby increasing total ownership costs above the minimum. However, under a replacement policy based on the observed level of O&S costs, total ownership costs are minimized because replacement only occurs when O&S costs reach the critical level.[3]

Our approach to deriving the cost-based optimality condition for the stochastic case is similar to that found in Manne (1961). As in Manne's capacity expansion example, we frame aircraft replacement as a "first passage" problem. In our case, O&S costs rise over time to a critical level, signaling that another replacement is optimal.[4]

Equation (11) is the expected total cost expression:

---

[3]The difference in total ownership costs between the age-based and cost-based replacement policies represents the value of knowing the actual level of O&S costs and having the ability to act on that knowledge. This cost difference might also be described as an option value, because the ability to delay replacement until O&S costs reach a critical level is similar to a financial option that the holder will not exercise unless the price of the underlying asset reaches a critical level. As with the financial option, the value of the option to delay replacement increases with the level of uncertainty.

[4]As above, we call the present-value O&S costs $M(x; m)$, let x go to infinity, and write the present value of life-cycle O&S costs as a recursive Bellman equation. However, in the stochastic model there is a significant difference. Here, we take the *expectation* of the differential of the life-cycle O&S costs because they are stochastic, so that $M(x; m) = mda + e^{-rda}[M(x; m) + E\{dM(x; m)\}]$, and we use Ito's Lemma to write the expected differential $dM(x; m)$.

$$c(x)=\frac{p+\dfrac{b\left[1-\left(\dfrac{b}{x}\right)^{\beta_1-1}\right]}{r-\alpha}}{1-\left(\dfrac{b}{x}\right)^{\beta_1}} \tag{11}$$

where $(b/x)^{\beta_1}$ is the expected discount factor and β_1 is the positive solution to the quadratic characteristic equation, $\frac{1}{2}\sigma^2(\beta-1)\beta+\alpha\beta-r=0$. For a discussion of this characteristic equation, see Appendix A.

Equation (12) is the new optimality condition:

$$x^*=\frac{\beta_1}{\beta_1-1}(r-\alpha)p+\frac{\beta_1}{\beta_1-1}(r-\alpha)\frac{\dfrac{b\left[1-\left(\dfrac{b}{x^*}\right)^{\beta_1-1}\right]}{r-\alpha}+p\left(\dfrac{b}{x^*}\right)^{\beta_1}}{1-\left(\dfrac{b}{x^*}\right)^{\beta_1}} \tag{12}$$

Equations (11) and (12) provide the stochastic counterparts to Eqs. (7) and (8).

By way of comparison, we note that the deterministic optimality condition, shown in Eq. (6), balanced the marginal costs and savings of delaying replacement by a small increment of time or age. Here, however, the optimality condition balances the costs and savings from waiting until instantaneous O&S costs increase by a small increment. In the deterministic example, the length of the delay was certain, while in the stochastic example, the length of the delay is random.

The two terms on the RHS of Eq. (12) represent the expected savings on the purchase of the immediate replacement and the expected savings on the expected discounted costs of all future O&S and replacement costs. In this case, the discount rate is $(\beta_1/(\beta_1-1))\,(r-\alpha)$ whereas in the deterministic case the discount rate is r. However, we can show numerically that as the variance in O&S cost growth rate goes to zero, the stochastic discount rate approaches r. As in the deterministic case, the second term on the RHS of Eq. (12) drops out for a single or one-time replacement.

Before proceeding to the graphical and numerical illustrations, we provide the crosswalk to the expected age at replacement. We find that examining the optimal replacement policy in terms of O&S cost levels provides little intuition as to how long the USAF can expect to keep its aircraft because the optimal replacement policy depends on the growth rate α. For high growth rates, a high level of O&S costs may imply a shorter expected replacement interval than a lower level of O&S costs at a lower growth rate. Thus, the expected age at replacement gives a better sense of how a cost-based replacement policy will actually play out over time.

Following the approach previewed in our discussion of deterministic O&S costs, we derive an expression for the expected age at which O&S costs will reach the replacement level, $a(x)$.[5] For the expected first passage time of O&S costs from their initial level b to some replacement level x:

$$a(x) = \frac{\ln\left(\frac{x}{b}\right)}{\alpha - \frac{1}{2}\sigma^2} \tag{13}$$

The derivation of this equation can be found in Appendix A. The only difference between this crosswalk and the deterministic crosswalk is the negative $1/2\sigma^2$ term in the denominator. All else constant, the expected age shown in Eq. (13) is always greater than the age shown in Eq. (9). We can see plainly here that the addition of the diffusion process results in a longer optimal replacement interval. When the variance goes to zero, this expected age expression converges to the age expression found in the deterministic case.

Graphical and Numerical Illustrations

As in the deterministic case, we can solve for x^* both graphically and numerically. First, we obtain the solution graphically by plotting the expected total cost equation as a function of x. Figure 5 illustrates the procedure for $\sigma =$ 0.10, $\sigma = 0.05$, and $\sigma = 0$. In each example, $\alpha = 0.025$, $r = 0.03$, $p/b = 50$, and $b = 1$, an index. For $\sigma = 0.05$, the optimal level of instantaneous O&S costs at replacement is about 3.7 times the initial level. For $\sigma = 0.10$, the optimal level rises to about four times the initial level. To aid in interpretation, we have included the expected age at first passage, $E\{a^*\}$, for each minimum. With some uncertainty, i.e., $\sigma = 0.05$ or $\sigma = 0.10$, the optimal policy would have the USAF holding its aircraft slightly longer than it did when the growth rate was certain, i.e., $\sigma = 0$, but the expected total cost would be somewhat lower.[6]

Although not as clearly depicted in Figure 5 as in the earlier figures, owing to the difference in vertical scales, the USAF has even more leeway in selecting a

[5]Our approach is similar to Karlin and Taylor (1981), pp. 191–193.

[6]Like the holder of a financial option, the USAF can, in effect, reduce its expected total ownership costs by waiting to see whether it is on a "good" or "bad" path.

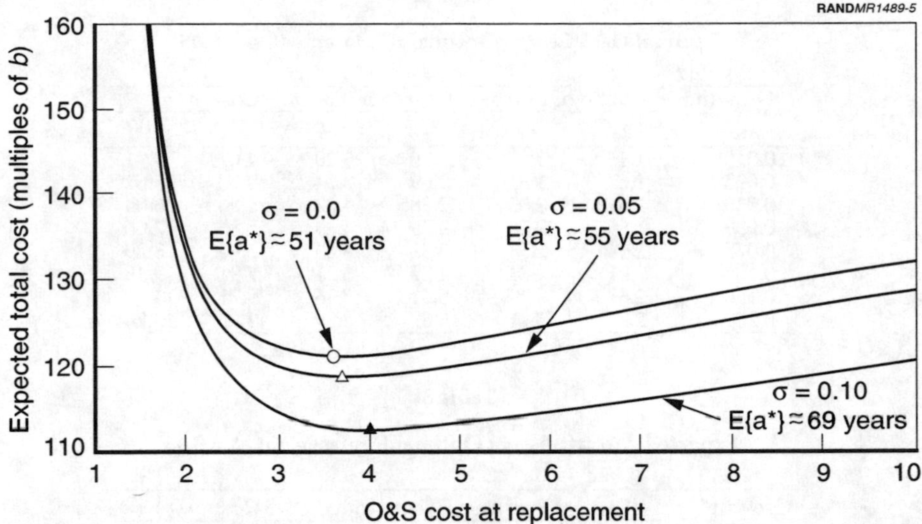

Figure 5—Graphical Solutions for the Cost-Based Model (Diffusion Process)

retirement interval. Recall, for $\alpha = 0.025$ and $\sigma = 0$, the effective window for remaining within 10 percent of the cost minimum was about 66 years; for $\sigma = 0.05$, the window is about 72 years, and for $\sigma = 0.10$, the window is about 89 years.

A table of solutions will make it easier to compare the results of the stochastic model with those of the deterministic model. We construct a set of tables for two levels of uncertainty: $\sigma = 0.05$ and $\sigma = 0.10$. To facilitate comparison, we begin by showing tables displaying the optimal O&S cost (Table 3a), the expected age at which that optimum is reached (Table 3b), the ratio of optimal O&S costs for the $\sigma = 0.05$ and $\sigma = 0$ cases (Table 3c), and the ratio of expected age at replacement to optimal replacement age for the $\sigma = 0.05$ and $\sigma = 0$ cases (Table 3d).[7]

It is clear that the optimal level of O&S costs at which a fleet should be replaced increases with uncertainty. Moreover, the uncertainty effect is stronger for lower expected growth rates and higher replacement costs (Table 3c).

Similarly, the expected age at optimal replacement increases with uncertainty, and the uncertainty effect is stronger at lower levels of the expected growth rate (Table 3d). On the other hand, the uncertainty effect is stronger at lower replacement costs when we are looking at expected age (Table 3d).

---

[7]The $\sigma = 0$ cases are the certainty cases.

Table 3a

Optimal O&S Cost at Optimal Replacement, $\sigma = 0.05$

Growth	Ratio of Purchase Cost to Initial O&S Cost (p/b)					
Rate, α	5	10	25	50	75	100
0.010	1.45	1.69	2.30	3.20	4.07	4.91
0.025	1.62	1.94	2.69	3.74	4.70	5.62
0.033	1.69	2.05	2.88	4.02	5.06	6.04
0.050	1.85	2.28	3.29	4.65	5.86	7.00
0.075	2.04	2.58	3.81	5.46	6.93	8.29
0.100	2.21	2.84	4.27	6.21	7.91	9.49
0.150	2.51	3.30	5.11	7.56	9.71	11.70
0.200	2.77	3.71	5.87	8.79	11.36	13.74

Table 3b

Expected Aircraft Age at Optimal Replacement, $\sigma = 0.05$

Growth	Ratio of Purchase Cost to Initial O&S Cost (p/b)					
Rate, α	5	10	25	50	75	100
0.010	42.41	60.25	95.25	133.04	160.30	181.96
0.025	20.23	27.81	41.66	55.57	65.20	72.70
0.033	16.83	22.94	33.84	44.56	51.88	57.55
0.050	12.62	16.94	24.41	31.53	36.28	39.92
0.075	9.69	12.83	18.12	23.03	26.25	28.68
0.100	8.05	10.56	14.71	18.49	20.94	22.79
0.150	6.19	8.02	10.97	13.60	15.28	16.54
0.200	5.14	6.59	8.91	10.94	12.23	13.18

Table 3c

Ratio of Optimal Replacement O&S Costs, $\sigma = 0.05/\sigma = 0$

Growth	Ratio of Purchase Cost to Initial O&S Cost (p/b)					
Rate, α	5	10	25	50	75	100
0.010	1.041	1.055	1.075	1.089	1.095	1.098
0.025	1.012	1.017	1.023	1.029	1.032	1.034
0.033	1.008	1.011	1.016	1.019	1.022	1.023
0.050	1.004	1.006	1.008	1.010	1.011	1.012
0.075	1.002	1.003	1.004	1.005	1.006	1.006
0.100	1.001	1.002	1.003	1.003	1.004	1.004
0.150	1.001	1.001	1.001	1.002	1.002	1.002
0.200	1.000	1.001	1.001	1.001	1.001	1.001

Next, we consider a higher level of uncertainty, $\sigma = 0.10$. Again, tables display the optimal O&S cost (Table 4a), the expected age at which that optimum is reached (Table 4b), the ratio of optimal O&S costs for the $\sigma = 0.10$ and $\sigma = 0$ cases (Table 4c), and the ratio of expected age at replacement to optimal replacement age for the $\sigma = 0.10$ and $\sigma = 0$ cases (Table 4d).

Table 3d

Ratio of Expected Aircraft Age at Optimal Replacement, $\sigma = 0.05/\sigma = 0$

Growth	Ratio of Purchase Cost to Initial O&S Cost (p/b)					
Rate, α	5	10	25	50	75	100
0.010	1.283	1.271	1.251	1.233	1.222	1.214
0.025	1.081	1.079	1.078	1.076	1.074	1.074
0.033	1.057	1.056	1.055	1.055	1.054	1.053
0.050	1.033	1.033	1.032	1.032	1.032	1.032
0.075	1.020	1.020	1.020	1.020	1.020	1.020
0.100	1.014	1.014	1.014	1.014	1.014	1.014
0.150	1.009	1.009	1.009	1.009	1.009	1.009
0.200	1.007	1.007	1.007	1.007	1.007	1.007

Table 4a

Optimal O&S Cost at Optimal Replacement, $\sigma = 0.10$

Growth	Ratio of Purchase Cost to Initial O&S Cost (p/b)					
Rate, α	5	10	25	50	75	100
0.010	1.56	1.86	2.62	3.73	4.79	5.83
0.025	1.67	2.02	2.86	4.04	5.12	6.15
0.033	1.73	2.11	3.01	4.25	5.38	6.45
0.050	1.87	2.32	3.37	4.79	6.06	7.26
0.075	2.06	2.60	3.85	5.55	7.05	8.45
0.100	2.22	2.85	4.31	6.27	8.00	9.60
0.150	2.52	3.31	5.13	7.60	9.76	11.77
0.200	2.78	3.71	5.89	8.82	11.40	13.79

Table 4b

Expected Aircraft Age at Optimal Replacement, $\sigma = 0.10$

Growth	Ratio of Purchase Cost to Initial O&S Cost (p/b)					
Rate, α	5	10	25	50	75	100
0.010	88.71	124.47	192.48	263.39	313.36	352.55
0.025	25.72	35.27	52.58	69.81	81.66	90.86
0.033	20.02	27.23	40.08	52.65	61.20	67.80
0.050	13.96	18.73	26.98	34.81	40.05	44.05
0.075	10.31	13.65	19.28	24.48	27.90	30.49
0.100	8.41	11.04	15.37	19.32	21.88	23.81
0.150	6.37	8.25	11.28	13.98	15.71	17.00
0.200	5.24	6.73	9.09	11.16	12.48	13.46

Tables 4c and 4d show that the optimal policy is much more affected by uncertainty at the $\sigma = 0.10$ level than it was at the $\sigma = 0.05$ level. The direction of the influence of the expected growth rate and replacement cost is the same.

Table 4c

Ratio of Optimal Replacement O&S Costs, σ = 0.10/σ = 0

Growth	Ratio of Purchase Cost to Initial O&S Cost (p/b)					
Rate, α	5	10	25	50	75	100
0.010	1.119	1.160	1.223	1.268	1.290	1.302
0.025	1.047	1.063	1.089	1.110	1.123	1.132
0.033	1.033	1.044	1.062	1.077	1.087	1.093
0.050	1.018	1.023	1.032	1.040	1.045	1.049
0.075	1.009	1.012	1.017	1.021	1.023	1.025
0.100	1.006	1.008	1.010	1.013	1.014	1.016
0.150	1.003	1.004	1.005	1.006	1.007	1.008
0.200	1.002	1.002	1.003	1.004	1.004	1.005

Table 4d

Ratio of Expected Aircraft Age at Optimal Replacement, σ = 0.10/σ = 0

Growth	Ratio of Purchase Cost to Initial O&S Cost (p/b)					
Rate, α	5	10	25	50	75	100
0.010	2.683	2.627	2.529	2.441	2.388	2.353
0.025	1.374	1.369	1.360	1.351	1.346	1.342
0.033	1.257	1.254	1.250	1.246	1.243	1.241
0.050	1.143	1.142	1.141	1.140	1.139	1.138
0.075	1.085	1.085	1.085	1.084	1.084	1.084
0.100	1.060	1.060	1.060	1.060	1.060	1.060
0.150	1.038	1.038	1.038	1.038	1.038	1.038
0.200	1.028	1.028	1.028	1.027	1.027	1.027

Incorporating uncertainty clearly changes the optimal replacement decision, but to what extent does it affect the USAF's economic objective—in this model, cost minimization? To calculate this, recall that the only parametric difference between the deterministic model and the stochastic diffusion model is the standard deviation in the O&S cost growth rate, σ. Because the deterministic approach does not include σ, it is as if that uncertainty is being ignored. Presumably, ignoring uncertainty would result in a suboptimal replacement policy, particularly when uncertainty is high. Stated slightly differently, incorporating uncertainty into the policy decision could provide cost savings in comparison to a replacement policy that ignores uncertainty.

To illustrate this point, Tables 5a and 5b show the percentage cost savings that the Air Force could obtain by following the stochastic cost-based optimal policy rather than the deterministic age-based optimal policy.

Just as the replacement effect increases with sigma, the cost savings also increase with sigma. When $\alpha = 0.025$ and $p/b = 50$, the cost savings are 2 percent for $\sigma =$

Table 5a

Expected Percentage Cost Savings from Incorporating Uncertainty, σ = 0.05

Growth	Ratio of Purchase Cost to Initial O&S Cost (p/b)					
Rate, α	5	10	25	50	75	100
0.010	5.8	4.6	2.7	1.5	0.9	0.6
0.025	3.5	3.1	2.5	2.0	1.7	1.5
0.033	2.9	2.6	2.2	1.9	1.6	1.5
0.050	2.0	1.9	1.7	1.5	1.4	1.3
0.075	1.4	1.4	1.3	1.2	1.1	1.1
0.100	1.1	1.1	1.0	0.9	0.9	0.9
0.150	0.8	0.7	0.7	0.7	0.7	0.6
0.200	0.6	0.6	0.5	0.5	0.5	0.5

Table 5b

Expected Percentage Cost Savings from Incorporating Uncertainty, σ = 0.10

Growth	Ratio of Purchase Cost to Initial O&S Cost (p/b)					
Rate, α	5	10	25	50	75	100
0.010	16.0	13.0	8.3	4.9	3.2	2.3
0.025	12.3	10.9	8.8	7.0	5.9	5.2
0.033	10.6	9.6	8.1	6.8	6.0	5.4
0.050	7.8	7.3	6.5	5.8	5.3	5.0
0.075	5.6	5.3	4.9	4.5	4.3	4.1
0.100	4.4	4.2	3.9	3.7	3.6	3.4
0.150	3.0	2.9	2.8	2.7	2.6	2.6
0.200	2.3	2.3	2.2	2.1	2.1	2.0

0.05; the cost savings rise to 7 percent for $\sigma = 0.10$. Although the cost savings increase consistently as replacement cost decreases for any given growth rate, they first increase and then decrease as the growth rate increases for any given level of replacement cost. (This pattern first emerges visibly in Table 5a when *p/b* reaches 50 and in Table 5b when p/b reaches 25.) Also, the growth rate at which that peak level of cost savings occurs appears to increase with the level of the replacement cost.

Discrete Upward Jumps in O&S Costs

We now add another stochastic term to the exponential process to account for the possibility of discrete upward jumps in O&S costs. Such a jump may occur, for example, if the sudden appearance of corrosion, a broken part, or some other potentially mission-impeding phenomenon requires additional inspections, yielding an upward shift in a generation's O&S cost curve. We specify this form of uncertainty as a Poisson jump process and add it to the diffusion process:[8]

$$dm = \alpha m da + \sigma m dz + m dq \tag{14}$$

The new term on the RHS of Eq. (14), *mdq*, characterizes the jump, where *dq* is the increment of the Poisson process. The jump increment can take two values: ϕ with a probability of $\lambda\, da$ and 0 with a probability of $1 - \lambda\, da$. As previously, the effects of uncertainty evolve proportionally with the age of the fleet.

Figure 6 illustrates the combined effect of the diffusion and the jump processes. It shows two of the infinitely many possible O&S cost realization paths. For comparative purposes, we set $\sigma = 0.05$, $\alpha = 0.025$, and $b = 1$, as previously in Figure 4, and "add" $\lambda = 0.05$ and $\phi = 0.50$ to incorporate the jump process.

Although not immediately obvious because of the difference in scales, the expected growth rate in Figure 6 is higher than in Figure 4. Adding the jump process raises the expected growth rate, all else constant, by $\lambda\,\phi$, so that the new rate is $\alpha + \lambda\phi$. For $\alpha = 0.025$, $\lambda = 0.05$, and $\phi = 0.50$, this amounts to an overall expected growth rate of 0.05, or twice the rate depicted in Figure 4.[9]

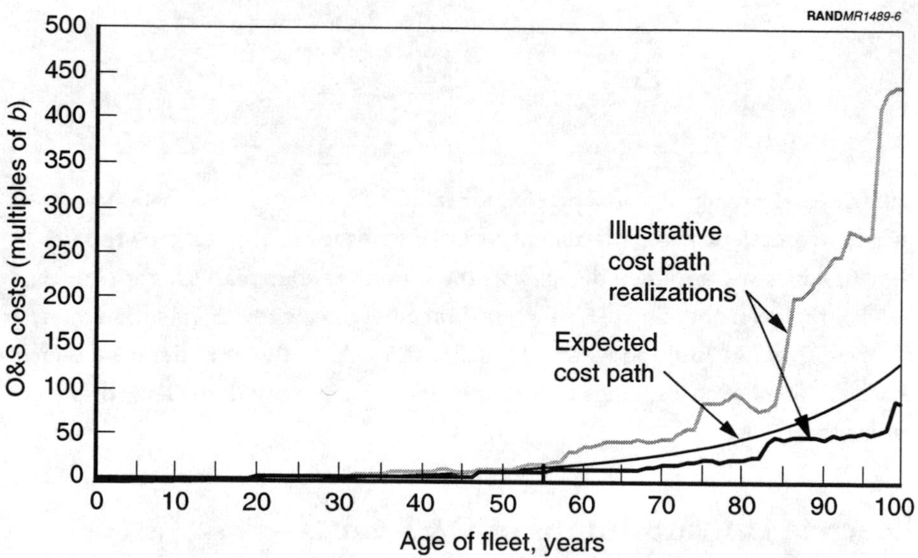

Figure 6—Two O&S Cost Path Realizations for the Jump-Diffusion Process

---

[8]See Dixit and Pindyck (1994), p. 85. Jump processes are often characterized as Poisson—"subject to jumps of fixed or random size, for which the arrival time follows a Poisson distribution."

[9]For a discussion of the expected growth rate, see Dixit and Pindyck (1994), p. 168.

Clearly, we could reduce α, λ, or ϕ to yield an overall rate of 0.025, but we show in the tables that follow that different combinations of parameters can produce different optimal policies even when the overall rate is the same.

Life-Cycle Costs and Optimality Conditions

As in the diffusion-only example, the instantaneous O&S cost level x is the decision variable for a cost-minimization policy. When instantaneous O&S costs rise above some critical level x^*, replacement is optimal.

Equation (15) is the new expected total cost expression:

$$c(x) = \frac{p + \dfrac{b\left[1 - \left(\dfrac{b}{x}\right)^{\beta_1' - 1}\right]}{r - \alpha - \lambda\phi}}{1 - \left(\dfrac{b}{x}\right)^{\beta_1'}} \tag{15}$$

where $(b/x)^{\beta_1'}$ is the expected discount factor and β_1' is the positive solution to the characteristic equation $\frac{1}{2}\sigma^2\beta'(\beta'-1) + \alpha\beta' - (r+\lambda) + \lambda(1+\phi)^{\beta'} = 0$.

Although the form of the expected discount factor for the jump-diffusion process is the same as for the diffusion process, the characteristic equation and its resulting root are different. Unlike the characteristic quadratic equation of the diffusion-only process, which can be solved analytically using the quadratic formula, the characteristic equation of the jump-diffusion must be solved numerically.

Note that as the variance and jump parameters in the jump-diffusion process go to zero, the expected discount factor approaches the deterministic discount factor e^{-ra} for an exponential growth process.

Equation (16) is the new optimality condition:

$$x^* = \frac{\beta_1'}{\beta_1' - 1}(r - \alpha - \lambda\phi)p + \frac{\beta_1'}{\beta_1' - 1}(r - \alpha - \lambda\phi)\frac{\dfrac{b\left[1 - \left(\dfrac{b}{x^*}\right)^{\beta_1' - 1}\right]}{r - \alpha - \lambda\phi} + p\left(\dfrac{b}{x^*}\right)^{\beta_1'}}{1 - \left(\dfrac{b}{x^*}\right)^{\beta_1'}} \tag{16}$$

Equations (15) and (16) provide counterparts to Eqs. (11) and (12). The two sets of equations look similar, but there are important differences. For the jump-diffusion process, the expected discount rate and life-cycle cost term reflect the arrival rate and magnitude of a jump. And, as noted above, β_1' and β_1, the positive roots of the jump-diffusion and diffusion-only characteristic equations, are different. Nevertheless, the basic interpretation of the optimality condition is the same—the optimality condition balances the expected marginal cost and benefit from waiting until instantaneous O&S costs increase by a small increment. All else constant, increasing the arrival rate or magnitude of upward jumps increases the expected total cost of owning a fleet of aircraft and decreases the expected age of the fleet at replacement.

For the jump-diffusion process, we can also provide a crosswalk to the expected age at first passage:

$$a(x) = \frac{\ln\left(\frac{x}{b}\right)}{\alpha - \frac{1}{2}\sigma^2 + \lambda \ln(1+\phi)} \tag{17}$$

This expected age expression is similar to the expression found for the diffusion process, except that the denominator is increased by the addition of a term reflective of the jump process. If we assume that the jump will always be positive, then, all else constant, the expected time to first passage of a jump-diffusion will always be less than the expected time to first passage of a diffusion-only process. When the variance goes to zero, the expected age at first passage for the "pure" jump process is:

$$a(x) = \frac{\ln\left(\frac{x}{b}\right)}{\alpha + \lambda \ln(1+\phi)} \tag{18}$$

Here, we see that the expected age is also less than in the deterministic case, where the expected age was $a(x) = \frac{1}{\alpha}\ln(\frac{x}{b})$. See Eq. (9).

The important point is that the diffusion and jump processes push the expected age in opposite and potentially offsetting directions. If both forms of uncertainty are present in a system, the outcome will depend on the relative strength of each process. As such, from a policy perspective, it is important to be able to qualitatively and quantitatively characterize the nature of uncertainty.

Graphical and Numerical Illustrations

As above, we can solve for x^* both graphically and numerically. Figure 7 presents comparative results for the jump-diffusion process, with $\sigma = 0.05$, $\lambda = 0.05$, and $\phi = 0.50$; the diffusion-only process, with $\sigma = 0.05$ and $\lambda = 0$; and the deterministic process, with $\sigma = 0$ and $\lambda = 0$. In each case, $\alpha = 0.025$, $r = 0.03$, $p/b = 50$, and $b = 1$, an index. To facilitate interpretation, we have included the results from the calculation of the expected age at first passage, $E\{a^*\}$, for each minimum.

With a jump, the optimal policy would have the USAF holding its aircraft until O&S costs reach a higher critical level than in either the diffusion-only or deterministic cases. Owing to the increase in the overall expected growth rate in O&S costs, the expected age at first passage would be substantially lower than in diffusion-only or deterministic cases. Moreover, the expected total cost would be higher. Also because of the increase in the overall expected growth rate, the USAF would have somewhat less latitude in selecting a replacement interval. For the case illustrated in Figure 7, costs would remain within 10 percent of the minimum for a period of about 33 years.

Next, we present numerical solutions. In Tables 6a and 6b, we choose combinations of α, λ, and ϕ to illustrate the effects of varying the arrival rate and the magnitude of the jump on the replacement interval for a fixed expected overall growth rate of O&S costs. To more readily identify the effects of the jump, we set $\sigma = 0$.

In Tables 6a and 6b, we see that as more of the expected overall growth rate comes from the magnitude of the jump, i.e., as ϕ increases and λ decreases, the

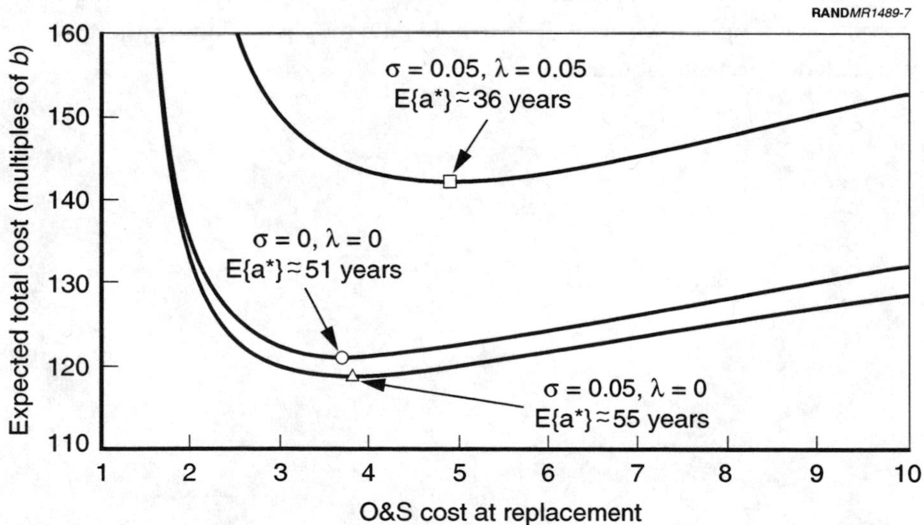

Figure 7—Graphical Solutions for the Cost-Based Model (Jump-Diffusion Process)

Table 6a

O&S Cost at Optimal Replacement, $\sigma = 0$

O&S Cost Growth Components				Ratio of Purchase Cost to Initial O&S Cost (p/b)					
α	λ	ϕ	Total	5	10	25	50	75	100
0.025	1.000	0.025	0.05	1.84	2.27	3.27	4.62	5.82	6.94
0.025	0.500	0.050	0.05	1.85	2.28	3.27	4.63	5.83	6.96
0.025	0.100	0.250	0.05	1.86	2.30	3.32	4.71	5.95	7.11
0.025	0.050	0.500	0.05	1.88	2.32	3.37	4.80	6.07	7.27
0.025	0.025	1.000	0.05	1.90	2.37	3.45	4.94	6.28	7.53

Table 6b

Expected Age at Optimal Replacement, $\sigma = 0$

O&S Cost Growth Components				Ratio of Purchase Cost to Initial O&S Cost (p/b)					
α	λ	ϕ	Total	5	10	25	50	75	100
0.025	1.000	0.025	0.05	12.31	16.53	23.83	30.78	35.43	38.99
0.025	0.500	0.050	0.05	12.41	16.66	24.01	31.01	35.70	39.28
0.025	0.100	0.250	0.05	13.12	17.60	25.36	32.74	37.68	41.45
0.025	0.050	0.500	0.05	13.89	18.63	26.84	34.63	39.83	43.81
0.025	0.025	1.000	0.05	15.17	20.35	29.28	37.75	43.40	47.71

critical level of O&S costs increases and the expected age at first passage also increases. Although not shown in either table, the minimized expected total cost also decreases with λ. This result is consistent with the notion that as jumps become less frequent, we are willing to hold onto the aircraft longer and the associated expected cost drops.

5. Policy Implications and Future Research

In the foregoing analysis, traditional asset replacement models and stochastic innovations suggest a framework for identifying optimal, i.e., cost-minimizing and expected-cost-minimizing, replacement strategies. We next discuss some of the implications of our parametric analysis and propose future research.

Policy Implications

When would it just be cheaper to replace old airplanes? By its very nature, a parametric analysis cannot provide a definitive answer, but the results do suggest that policymakers may have some leeway in choosing a replacement age. For low O&S cost growth rates, the USAF's total ownership costs stay within a narrow range of the minimum over extended periods. This leeway may be especially important if procurement budgets are constrained. As Smith (1957) suggests, a modest delay in the replacement of one fleet, albeit suboptimal, can free-up funds for other acquisitions. However, as the growth rate in O&S costs rises, or the effects of jumps become larger, this kind of financing becomes more costly, measured by the deviation from the least-cost solution. Were sufficient data available, we might be able to use them to estimate the USAF's implicit discount rate by comparing actual and seemingly optimal replacement decisions.

In the diffusion model, we find that uncertainty serves to lengthen the optimal replacement interval and reduce costs, but only slightly if the variance is low relative to the expected growth rate. However, as the variance grows, all else constant, the effects of the diffusion process become more pronounced and the cost associated with setting policy according to a simple deterministic model becomes greater. Consistent with Meyer (1971), this result suggests that the potential costs from failing to account for uncertainty will be greater in a high-variance system.

In the jump-diffusion model, the jump process serves to shorten the optimal replacement interval, possibly resulting in an even shorter interval than in the deterministic model. Consistent with intuition, the possibility of discrete upward jumps effectively increases the expected growth rate of O&S costs for the fleet and dampens the USAF's interest in holding it for an extended period. Moreover, different combinations of λ and ϕ can yield the same overall expected growth rate of O&S costs, but they lead to different optimal policies—the arrival rate and magnitude of the jump enter both the optimality condition and the expected age expression differently.[1]

In summary, we find that the diffusion and jump processes have opposing and potentially offsetting effects on the length of the optimal replacement interval. If both forms of uncertainty are present in the system, the net effect will depend on the relative strength of each process, where strength encompasses variance, arrival rate, and magnitude. Observing the tension between processes, we find it especially important to be able to characterize the nature of the uncertainty—both qualitatively and quantitatively. It is not enough to say the USAF faces uncertainty, rather it is essential to ask "what kind?" and "how much?" To accomplish this characterization, more detailed data on military aircraft costs, particularly by tail number, would be helpful. Absent such data, it may be possible to draw insight from publicly available data on commercial aircraft.

Future Research

The foregoing discussion suggests several opportunities for future research. Among them, we intend to explore the implications of model specification (e.g., convex, linear, and concave growth functions) and, to the extent possible, compare their merits on empirical grounds. We are interested in investigating the effects of functional form on both total ownership costs and the replacement interval. We will seek validation from both military and commercial data in our assessment of the models' empirical merits.

In future work, we intend to add several "real world" features. First, we will disaggregate O&S costs into subcategories, such as organizational maintenance, depot-level reparables, engine overhaul and rework, airframe overhaul and rework, and other costs, including personnel and energy. Only some of these categories will exhibit age-dependent growth. Next, we will add order delivery lags and time-phased replacements. We will also experiment with different kinds of uncertainty, including processes that account for spikes (sudden short-lived cost increases), permanent institutional shifts, and fluctuating purchase prices. Finally, we will investigate the effects of technological improvements.

---

[1]The difference in the roles of λ and ϕ in the optimality condition is not immediately obvious from Eq. (16), but it is apparent in the characteristic equation.

Appendix

A. Solution Methodology

This appendix illustrates the solution methodology.

In the main body of the text, we present an expression for expected total present-value ownership cost, Eq. (11):

$$c(x) = \frac{p + \frac{b\left[1 - \left(\frac{b}{x}\right)^{\beta_1 - 1}\right]}{r - \alpha}}{1 - \left(\frac{b}{x}\right)^{\beta_1}} \tag{11}$$

Expected total present-value ownership cost can be decomposed into three expressions: replacement cost, expected present-value life-cycle O&S cost, and expected discount factor at replacement. Although the replacement cost is simply a constant, p, the other two expressions may be less familiar to some readers. We also present an expression for expected age at replacement, Eq. (13), which similarly may be less familiar:

$$a(x) = \frac{\ln\left(\frac{x}{b}\right)}{\alpha - \frac{1}{2}\sigma^2} \tag{13}$$

In this appendix, we show the derivation of the expressions for the expected present-value life-cycle O&S cost, the expected discount factor at replacement, and the expected age at replacement. Although we derive expressions only for the case in which O&S costs evolve as a geometric Brownian motion, Eq. (10),

$$dm = \alpha m da + \sigma m dz \tag{10}$$

the methodology is applicable to the deterministic and jump-diffusion ownership cost and replacement age expressions presented in the text.

Our approach in all cases is similar: We derive and solve a differential equation describing the evolution of the function in which we are interested. We begin by writing a recursive Bellman equation that incorporates the expected differential of the function along with any relevant discount factor or instantaneous costs or changes. Next, we expand the function differential using a Taylor series expansion, for deterministic cost growth, or Ito's lemma, for stochastic cost growth. After substituting the expectation of the expanded differential back into the Bellman equation, we take the limit as the age increment goes to zero to get the differential equation. Using standard methods, we find the form of solution for the differential equation and any particular solutions, if necessary. Finally, we apply boundary conditions to obtain functional expressions for the expected age at replacement, the expected discount factor at replacement, and the expected present-value life-cycle O&S cost. The three functional expressions are derived below.

Expected Age at Replacement

We derive an expression for the expected age, $a(x;m)$, at which instantaneous O&S costs first evolve from their current level m to the policy-determined replacement level x. To reduce notational clutter, note that we will not use an expectation operator with $a(x;m)$, although we will use it everywhere else it would be appropriate.

We begin the derivation by writing a recursive Bellman equation for the evolution of $a(x;m)$. The Bellman equation consists of two terms: The first term represents the gain in expected age at replacement that accrues during the current age increment; the second term represents the expected age at replacement at the end of the current age increment. Note that the age increment da equates to the passage of calendar time, while $da(x;m)$ equates to the passage of O&S costs:

$$a(x;m) = da + (a(x;m) + E\{da(x;m)\})$$

Modify the Bellman equation by subtracting $a(x;m)$ from both sides and dividing through by da:

$$\frac{E\{da(x;m)\}}{da} + 1 = 0$$

Since $E\{da(x;m)\}$ is a function of the stochastic process followed by O&S costs, we expand it using Ito's lemma:

$$E\{da(x;m)\} = E\left\{\frac{da(x;m)}{dm}dm + \frac{1}{2}\frac{d^2a(x;m)}{dm^2}(dm)^2\right\}$$

Substituting for dm and taking the expectations gives an expression for the expected differential of the first passage age:

$$E\{da(x;m)\} = \left(\frac{1}{2}\sigma^2 m^2 \frac{d^2 a(x;m)}{dm^2} + \alpha m \frac{da(x;m)}{dm} \right) da$$

Substitute this expression for $E\{da(x;m)\}$ into the modified Bellman equation to get the second-order nonhomogenous differential equation for expected age. We do not need to take the limit as the age increment *da* goes to zero because the age increments cancel when we substitute for $E\{da(x;m)\}$.

$$\frac{1}{2}\sigma^2 m^2 \frac{d^2 a(x;m)}{dm^2} + \alpha m \frac{da(x;m)}{dm} + 1 = 0$$

The general solution for this type of differential equation has a well-known form:

$$a(x;m) = A + B\ln(m)$$

Substitute the assumed solution into the differential equation and perform the differentiations to solve for the constant B:

$$-\frac{1}{2}\sigma^2 m^2 \frac{B}{m^2} + \alpha m \frac{B}{m} + 1 = 0 \Rightarrow B = -\frac{1}{\alpha - \frac{1}{2}\sigma^2}$$

The boundary condition states that the expected age at which O&S costs reach their replacement level, starting from the replacement level, is zero. Apply this boundary condition, when $m = x$, to solve for the constant A:

$$a(x;x) = 0 = A - \frac{\ln(x)}{\alpha - \frac{1}{2}\sigma^2} \Rightarrow A = \frac{\ln(x)}{\alpha - \frac{1}{2}\sigma^2}$$

Substitute this expression for the constant A in the general form of solution to obtain the expression for the expected age at which O&S costs first evolve from their current level m to the replacement level x. Since the current level of O&S costs at the beginning of a generation life cycle is b, the expected age at which a generation of aircraft is replaced is:

$$a(x;b) = \frac{\ln\left(\frac{x}{b}\right)}{\alpha - \frac{1}{2}\sigma^2}$$

Expected Discount Factor at Replacement

We next derive an expression for the expected discount factor $f(x;m)$, which applies when instantaneous O&S costs first evolve from their current level m

to the policy-determined replacement level x. The semicolon distinguishes the decision variable x from the state variable m. As in the previous section, we write $f(x;m)$ without the expectation operator. We could also write this function as $E\{e^{-ra(x;m)}\}$, but note that in this case $a(x;m)$ is not an expectation but the realized age. Begin the derivation by writing a recursive Bellman equation for the evolution of $f(x;m)$:

$$f(x;m) = e^{-rda}(f(x;m) + E\{df(x;m)\})$$

In this case, the Bellman equation consists of only one term, which discounts the value of the function one increment of age in the future. There is no term for immediate cumulation, as there is in the last section for age or in the next section for costs, because the discount factor changes multiplicatively, rather than additively, over time. Rearrange the Bellman equation by subtracting $f(x;m)$ from both sides and dividing both sides by the discount factor:

$$E\{df(x;m)\} + (1 - e^{rda})f(x;m) = 0$$

Since $E\{df(x;m)\}$ is a function of the stochastic process followed by O&S costs, we expand it using Ito's lemma, substitute for dm, and take the expectation:

$$E\{df(x;m)\} = \left(\frac{1}{2}\sigma^2 m^2 \frac{d^2 f(x;m)}{dm^2} + \alpha m \frac{df(x;m)}{dm}\right) da$$

Substitute the expected differential back into the rearranged Bellman equation, divide both sides by da, and take the limit as da goes to zero to obtain the second-order homogeneous differential equation for the expected discount factor:

$$\frac{1}{2}\sigma^2 m^2 \frac{d^2 f(x;m)}{dm^2} + \alpha m \frac{df(x;m)}{dm} - rf(x;m) = 0$$

The general solution for this type of differential equation, a Cauchy-Euler differential equation, has a well-known form:

$$f(x;m) = Am^{\beta_1} + Bm^{\beta_2}$$

We will find expressions for the constants A and B by applying boundary conditions. The exponents β_1 and β_2 are the positive and negative roots of the characteristic quadratic equation, which can be found by substituting m^{β} into the differential equation:

$$\frac{1}{2}\sigma^2(\beta - 1)\beta + \alpha\beta - r = 0$$

Solve for β_1 and β_2 by using the quadratic formula

$$\beta = -\left(\frac{\alpha}{\sigma^2} - \frac{1}{2}\right) \pm \sqrt{\left(\frac{\alpha}{\sigma^2} - \frac{1}{2}\right)^2 + \frac{2r}{\sigma^2}}$$

The first boundary condition states that as the current level of O&S costs goes to zero, the time until O&S costs reach their critical level goes to infinity and the expected discount factor goes to zero:

$$f(x;0) = 0 = A0^{\beta_1} + B0^{\beta_2}$$

Since β_2 is negative, the second term goes to infinity as m goes to zero. To satisfy the boundary condition, set $B = 0$. The second boundary condition states that when the current level of O&S cost equals the replacement level, the time until O&S costs reach that level goes to zero and the expected discount factor goes to one:

$$f(x;x) = 1 = Ax^{\beta_1} \Rightarrow A = x^{-\beta_1}$$

Substitute the expressions for *A* and *B* back into the form of solution for the differential equation to obtain the expression for the expected discount factor at first passage of O&S costs from the current level of *m* to the replacement level *x*:

$$f(m) = \left(\frac{m}{x}\right)^{\beta_1}$$

Expected Present-Value Life-Cycle Cost

Finally, we derive an expression for the expected present-value sum of O&S costs incurred during an aircraft generation life cycle, $M(x;m)$. The written form of the function $M(x;m)$ is meant to be read as follows: the value of the function *M* when O&S costs have evolved from their current level *m* to the policy-determined replacement level *x*. Begin the derivation by writing a recursive Bellman equation for the evolution of $M(x;m)$:

$$M(x;m) = mda + e^{-rda}(M(x;m) + E\{dM(x;m)\})$$

The Bellman equation consists of two terms: the O&S costs that accrue during the current small age increment, and all future expected O&S costs discounted back from the end of the age increment. Rearrange the Bellman equation by subtracting $M(x;m)$ from both sides, dividing both sides by the discount factor, and then dividing both sides by the age increment:

$$\frac{E\{dM(x;m)\}}{da} + \left(\frac{1 - e^{rda}}{da}\right)M(x;m) + me^{rda} = 0$$

Since $E\{dM(x;m)\}$ is a function of the stochastic process followed by m, we expand it using Ito's lemma, substitute for dm, and take the expectation:

$$E\{dM(x;m)\} = \left(\frac{1}{2}\sigma^2 m^2 \frac{d^2M(x;m)}{dm^2} + \alpha m \frac{dM(x;m)}{dm}\right)da$$

Substitute the expected differential back into the rearranged Bellman equation and take the limit as da goes to zero to obtain the second-order nonhomogeneous differential equation for the expected present-value life-cycle cost:

$$\frac{1}{2}\sigma^2 m^2 \frac{d^2M(x;m)}{dm^2} + \alpha m \frac{dM(x;m)}{dm} - rM(x;m) + m = 0$$

The general solution for this type of differential equation, a Cauchy-Euler differential equation, has the well-known form:

$$M(x;m) = Am^{\beta_1} + Bm^{\beta_2} + part(m)$$

where $part(m)$ are any particular solutions, the constants A and B will be determined by the boundary conditions, and β_1 and β_2 are the positive and negative roots of the same characteristic quadratic equation as in the previous section. Particular solutions can be found by substituting e^z for m as the independent variable and then using the method of undetermined coefficients:

$$part(m) = \frac{m}{r-\alpha}$$

The particular solution can be thought of as the fundamental component of life-cycle O&S costs, in that it describes the present value of the flow of O&S costs over an infinite horizon.

Finding the two constants A and B in the general form of solution to the differential equation of present-value life-cycle O&S costs requires application of two boundary conditions. These boundary conditions describe the behavior of $M(x;m)$ when the current level of O&S costs is zero and when it reaches the replacement level x. Because zero is an absorbing point of the geometric Brownian motion followed by O&S costs, if instantaneous O&S costs ever drop to zero they will remain there forever. In that case, the expected present value of life-cycle O&S costs is zero because no O&S costs will ever be incurred:

$$M(x;0) = A(0)^{\beta_1} + B(0)^{\beta_2} + \frac{(0)}{r-\alpha} = 0$$

Because $\beta_2 < 0$, as O&S costs go to zero the second term in the solution goes to infinity. To satisfy the boundary condition, set $B = 0$. When O&S costs reach the level at which replacement occurs, x, life-cycle costs go to zero because the life cycle has ended:

$$M(x;x) = Ax^{\beta_1} + \frac{x}{r-\alpha} = 0 \Rightarrow A = -\frac{x\left(\frac{1}{x}\right)^{\beta_1}}{r-\alpha}$$

Substitute for A and B in the general solution and rearrange to get the expression for the expected present value of life-cycle O&S costs. Because the current level of O&S costs at the beginning of a generation life cycle is b, the expected present value of life-cycle O&S costs is

$$M(x;b) = \frac{b\left(1-\left(\frac{b}{x}\right)^{\beta_1-1}\right)}{r-\alpha}$$

B. Interest Rate Sensitivity

Tables B.1–B.4 provide numerical solutions for s* in the deterministic age-based model, for interest rates ranging from 0.01 to 0.10. Table B.2 corresponds to Table 1 in the main body of the text.

Table B.1

Interest Rate Sensitivity, $r = 0.01$

Growth	Ratio of Purchase Cost to Initial O&S Cost (p/b)					
Rate, α	5	10	25	50	75	100
0.010	30.04	41.62	63.27	85.77	101.82	114.62
0.025	17.73	24.01	35.11	45.93	53.31	59.01
0.033	15.08	20.28	29.31	37.98	43.82	48.30
0.050	11.80	15.69	22.31	28.51	32.62	35.74
0.075	9.25	12.17	17.03	21.48	24.38	26.57
0.100	7.76	10.13	14.02	17.52	19.79	21.48
0.150	6.04	7.79	10.61	13.10	14.69	15.87
0.200	5.03	6.44	8.67	10.62	11.86	12.77

Table B.2

Interest Rate Sensitivity, $r = 0.03$

Growth	Ratio of Purchase Cost to Initial O&S Cost (p/b)					
Rate, α	5	10	25	50	75	100
0.010	33.07	47.39	76.12	107.92	131.20	149.85
0.025	18.72	25.77	38.66	51.66	60.68	67.72
0.033	15.93	21.71	32.06	42.26	49.23	54.63
0.050	12.22	16.40	23.64	30.54	35.16	38.69
0.075	9.50	12.58	17.77	22.57	25.73	28.12
0.100	7.93	10.41	14.50	18.23	20.65	22.47
0.150	6.14	7.95	10.87	13.47	15.14	16.39
0.200	5.10	6.55	8.85	10.86	12.14	13.10

Table B.3

Interest Rate Sensitivity, $r = 0.05$

Growth Rate, α	Ratio of Purchase Cost to Initial O&S Cost (p/b) 5	10	25	50	75	100
0.010	36.62	54.32	91.37	132.14	160.94	183.26
0.025	19.80	27.73	42.67	58.02	68.70	76.99
0.033	16.53	22.83	34.37	45.93	53.86	59.99
0.050	12.65	17.15	25.08	32.73	37.87	41.81
0.075	9.76	13.01	18.55	23.73	27.16	29.75
0.100	8.11	10.70	15.01	18.96	21.54	23.49
0.150	6.24	8.11	11.15	13.86	15.61	16.91
0.200	5.17	6.65	9.02	11.11	12.44	13.42

Table B.4

Interest Rate Sensitivity, $r = 0.10$

Growth Rate, α	Ratio of Purchase Cost to Initial O&S Cost (p/b) 5	10	25	50	75	100
0.010	47.60	74.72	128.40	181.23	221.06	238.20
0.025	22.92	33.42	53.69	73.82	87.14	97.11
0.033	18.67	26.65	41.72	56.63	66.54	73.98
0.050	13.86	19.25	29.01	38.50	44.80	49.56
0.075	10.45	14.17	20.66	26.80	30.85	33.90
0.100	8.58	11.46	16.36	20.91	23.88	26.11
0.150	6.50	8.53	11.87	14.87	16.81	18.26
0.200	5.35	6.93	9.48	11.74	13.19	14.26

References

Alchian, Armen (1952), *Economic Replacement Policy*, RAND, R-224.

Alchian, Armen (1958), *Economic Replacement Policy*, RAND, RM-2153.

Bellman, Richard (1955), "Equipment Replacement Policy," *Journal of the Society for Industrial and Applied Mathematics*, Vol. 3, No. 3, pp. 133–136.

Boness, A. James, and Arnold N. Schwartz (1969), "A Cost-Benefit Analysis of Military Aircraft Replacement Policies," *Naval Research Logistics Quarterly*, Vol. 16, No. 2, pp. 237–257.

Clark, Colin W. (1990), "Chapter 8: Growth and Aging," in *Mathematical Bioeconomics: The Optimal Management of Renewable Resources*, 2nd ed., Wiley, New York.

Didonato, Mike, and Greg Sweers (1997), "The Economic Considerations of Operating Post Production Aircraft Beyond Design Service Objectives," The Boeing Company, Airplane Economic Analysis Group, presented at the Aircraft Heavy Maintenance and Upgrades Conference.

Dixit, Avinash K., and Robert S. Pindyck (1994), *Investment Under Uncertainty*, Princeton University Press, New Jersey.

Dreyfus, Stuart E. (1960), "A Generalized Equipment Replacement Study," *Journal of the Society for Industrial and Applied Mathematics*, Vol. 8, No. 3, pp. 425–435.

Faustmann, Martin (1849), "Calculation of the Value Which Forest Land and Immature Stands Possess for Forestry," first published in German, *Allegmeine Forst- und Jagd-Zeitung*, December 15, pp. 441–455, and translated into English by M. Gane (1968), "Martin Faustmann and the Evolution of Discounted Cash Flow," two articles from the original German of 1849, Institute Paper No. 42, Commonwealth Forestry Institute, University of Oxford.

Feller, William (1957), *An Introduction to Probability Theory and Its Applications*, Vol. 1, 2nd ed., Wiley, New York.

Gane, M. (1968), "Martin Faustmann and the Evolution of Discounted Cash Flow," two articles from the original German of 1849, Institute Paper No. 42, Commonwealth Forestry Institute, University of Oxford.

Hartwick, John M., and Nancy Olewiler (1985), "Chapter 11: Forestry Use," in *The Economics of Natural Resource Use*, Addison-Wesley Educational Publications, Boston.

Hertzler, Greg (1991), "Dynamic Decisions Under Risk: Application of Ito Stochastic Control in Agriculture," *American Journal of Agricultural Economics*, pp. 1126–1137.

Hildebrandt, Gregory G. (1980), *The Economics of Military Capital*, RAND, R-2665-AF.

Hildebrandt, Gregory G., and Manbing Sze (1990), *An Estimation of USAF Aircraft Operating and Support Cost Relations,* RAND, N-3062-ACQ.

Hotelling, Harold (1925), "A General Mathematical Theory of Depreciation," *Journal of the American Statistical Association*, Vol. 20, Issue 151, pp. 340–353.

Hunter, Duncan (1999), *Statement of Honorable Duncan Hunter, Chairman, Military Procurement Subcommittee*, Military Procurement Subcommittee, House Armed Services Committee, U.S. Congress, Hearing on Aging Equipment, Washington, D.C.

Karlin, Samuel, and Howard M. Taylor (1975), *A First Course in Stochastic Processes*, 2nd ed., Academic Press, New York.

Karlin, Samuel, and Howard M. Taylor (1981), *A Second Course in Stochastic Processes*, Academic Press, New York.

Manne, Alan S. (1961), "Capacity Expansion and Probabilistic Growth," *Econometrica*, Vol. 29, No. 4, pp. 632–649.

Marks, Kenneth E., and Ronald W. Hess (1981), *Estimating Aircraft Depot Maintenance Costs*, RAND, R-2731-PA&E.

Meyer, Robert A., Jr. (1971), "Equipment Replacement Under Uncertainty," *Management Science*, Vol. 17, No. 11, pp. 750–758.

Miller, Robert A., and Karl Voltaire (1983), "A Stochastic Analysis of the Tree Paradigm," *Journal of Economic Dynamics and Control*, Vol. 6, pp. 371–386.

National Research Council (1997), *Aging of U.S. Air Force Aircraft*, Final Report, Committee on Aging of U.S. Air Force Aircraft, National Materials Advisory Board, Commission on Engineering and Technical Systems, and National Research Council, publication NMAB-488-2, National Academy Press, Washington, D.C.

Office of Management and Budget (2001), Circular No. A-94, downloaded May 28.

Oksendal, Bernt (1998), *Stochastic Differential Equations: An Introduction with Applications*, Springer, Berlin.

Peters, F. Whitten (2000), "Readiness Challenges of Today's Air Force," September 13 remarks to the Air Force Association National Convention, Washington, D.C., available at http://www.af.mil/news/speech/current/spch29.html.

Pierrot, Lane (1999), *Statement of Lane Pierrot, Senior Analyst, National Security Division, Congressional Budget Office*, testifying before the Military Procurement Subcommittee, House Armed Services Committee, U.S. Congress, February 24 Hearing on Aging Equipment, Washington, D.C.

Preinreich, Gabriel A.D. (1940), "The Economic Life of Industrial Equipment," *Econometrica*, Vol. 8, Issue 1, pp. 12–44.

Pyles, Raymond (1999), *Statement of Dr. Raymond A. Pyles Before the Procurement Subcommittee of the House Armed Services Committee*, February 24; reprinted as *Aging Aircraft: Implications for Programmed Depot Maintenance and Engine-Support Costs*, RAND, CT-149.

Ryan, General Michael (2000), then U.S. Air Force Chief of Staff, quoted in John A. Tirpak,
"A Clamor for Airlift," *Air Force Magazine*, Vol. 83, No. 12.

Schwartz, Arnold N., James A. Sheler, and Carl R. Cooper (1971), "Dynamic Programming Approach to the Optimization of Naval Aircraft Rework and Replacement Strategies," *Naval Research Logistics Quarterly*, Vol. 18, No. 3, pp. 395–414.

Smith, Vernon L. (1957), "Economic Equipment Policies: An Evaluation," *Management Science*, Vol. 4, No. 1, October, pp. 20–37.

Taylor, J. S. (1923), "A Statistical Theory of Depreciation," *Journal of the American Statistical Association*, Vol. 18, Issue 144, pp. 1010–1023.

Tirpak, John A. (2000), "A Clamor for Airlift," *Air Force Magazine*, Vol. 83, No. 12.

U.S. Congressional Budget Office (2001), *The Effects of Aging on the Costs of Operating and Maintaining Military Equipment*, Washington, D.C.

U.S. General Accounting Office (1996), *U.S. Combat Air Power, Aging Refueling Aircraft Are Costly to Maintain and Operate*, GAO/NSIAD-96-160, Washington, D.C.

U.S. General Accounting Office (2000a), *Military Readiness, Air Transport Capability Falls Short of Requirements*, GAO/NSIAD-00-135, Washington, D.C.

U.S. General Accounting Office (2000b), *Defense Acquisitions, Air Force Operating and Support Cost Reductions Need Higher Priority*, GAO/NSIAD-00-165, Washington, D.C.

Willassen, Yngve (1998), "The Stochastic Rotation Problem: A Generalization of Faustmann's Formula to Stochastic Forest Growth," *Journal of Economic Dynamics and Control*, Vol. 22, pp. 573–596.

Wolf, Frank (2001), "Air Force Estimates Need for $500M to Fix Unanticipated Equipment Problems," *Defense Daily*.

Wolfram, Stephen (2001), *Mathematica*, version 4.1, Wolfram Research.